Presented To: S0-DYT-939

From:

date:

HAPPY BIRTHDAY!

HONOR H BOOKS

Inspiration and Motivation for the Seasons of Life

An Imprint of Cook Communications Ministries • Colorado Springs, CO

08 07 06 05 04   10 9 8 7 6 5 4 3 2 1

Happy Birthday!
ISBN 1-56292-176-2
Copyright © 2004 Bordon Books.
6532 E. 71 Street, Suite 105
Tulsa, OK 74133

Published by Honor Books
An Imprint of Cook Communications Ministries
4050 Lee Vance View
Colorado Springs, CO 80918

Developed by Bordon Books

Introduction

Happy Birthday! Though you may not always want people to know how old you are, it is your special day, and with it come great memories of birthdays past and dreams of many years to live life to the fullest.

On your special day, family and friends want you to know how much they love you, and how happy they are to celebrate YOU! To help you celebrate the day, we've put together a little book filled with motivational quotes to fuel your dreams, as well as interesting facts and trivia about birthdays in general and the month of your birthday in particular. We've also included birthday traditions developed by other families, and lots of fun ideas to inspire a wonderful celebration.

Since birthdays are a celebration of you as a total person, we've also added some inspirational verses from the Bible that remind you of how special you are. For when it comes to your birthday, no one is more excited to say "Happy Birthday!" than the God who made you, gave you special gifts and talents, and loves you dearly. So enjoy yourself on your special day, and don't forget to have a happy birthday!

Contents

Every person's life is

a fairy tale written

by God's fingers.

HAPPY BIRTHDAY!

Inspiration

The wiser mind mourns

less for what age takes away

than what it leaves behind.

Trust in Yourself and you are
Doomed to Disappointment. . . .
but trust in God,
and you are never to be confounded
in time or eternity.

A well-trained memory is one that permits you to forget everything that isn't worth remembering.

Carve your name

on hearts

and not on marble.

To me, old age is always fifteen years older than I am.

14

The course of human
history is determined,
not by what happens in the skies,
but by what takes place
in our hearts.

The ONLY preparation
for tomorrow is the
right Use of toDay.

Not in entire forgetfulness,

And not in utter nakedness,

But trailing clouds

of glory do we come

From God, who is our eternal home.

Never be afraid to trust

an unknown future

to a known God.

You can accomplish more

in one hour with God than

in one Lifetime without Him.

HAPPY BIRTHDAY!

People Do not change

with the times;

They change the times.

Middle age is when
you're faced with two temptations
and you choose the one
that will get you
home by nine o'clock.

Don't fear change—

embrace it.

Maturity doesn't
come with age;
it comes with acceptance
of responsibility.

You know you are getting old

when the candles

cost more than the cake.

At twenty years of age

the will reigns;

at thirty the wit;

at forty the judgement.

HAPPY BIRTHDAY!

The future lies before you,

like paths of pure, white snow.

Be careful how you tread it,

for every step

will show.

26

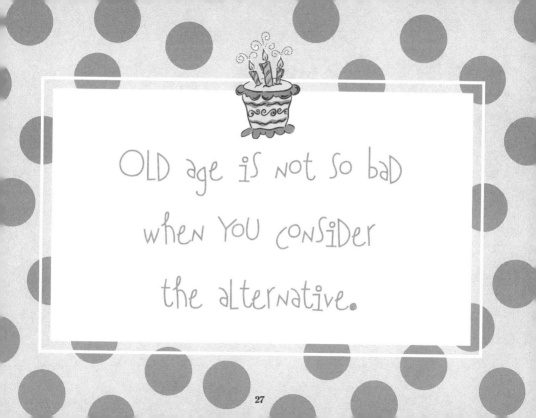

OLD age is not so bad
when YOU consider
the alternative.

The best things are nearest:

breath in your nostrils, light in your eyes,

flowers at your feet, duties at your hand,

the path of God just before you.

We live in deeds, not years;

in thoughts, not breaths.

We should count time by heartthrobs.

He most lives who thinks most—

feels the noblest—acts the best.

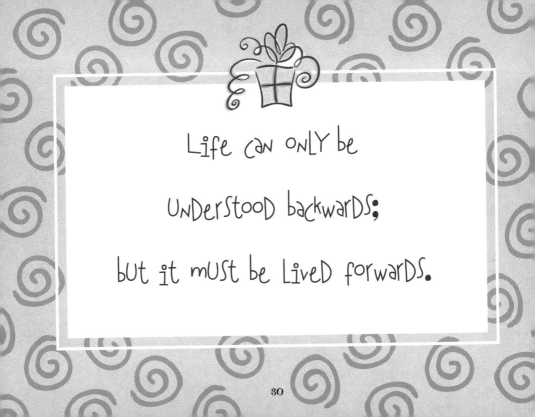

Life can only be

understood backwards;

but it must be lived forwards.

When you were born,

you cried and the world rejoiced.

Live your life in such a manner

that when you die

the world cries and you rejoice.

We make a living by
what we get—
we make a life
by what we give.

The value of life lies,

not in the length of days,

but in the use

we make of them.

HAPPY BIRTHDAY!

It is not by the

gray of the hair

that one knows the

age of the heart.

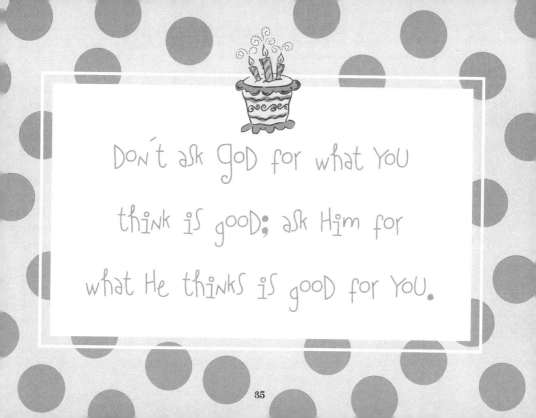

Don't ask God for what you think is good; ask Him for what He thinks is good for you.

I Like the Dreams of the future better than the history of the past.

HAPPY BIRTHDAY!

Trivia

Just For Kings

Centuries ago, only kings and royalty
were recognized as important enough
to have a birthday celebration.

Let the Children Party!

Children's birthday parties

originated in Germany

and were called kinderfeste.

Month of the Most Birthdays

August is the most
popular birthday month.

More people celebrate their
birthdays in August
than any other month.

Largest Party

The largest private birthday party

ever held was in 1970 for

Colonel Harlan Sanders'

eighty-ninth birthday.

Over 35,000 people attended the event.

HAPPY BIRTHDAY!

How Many Hours?

Go to this website and enter your
birth date and the current date
to find out how many days, hours,
and minutes old you are!

http://www.timeanddate.com/
date/duration.html

Cakes and Candles

Some claimed that it was really the Germans who invented birthday cakes, and celebrated birthdays with a cake called geburtstagorten. The Germans, also known to have been skilled candlemakers, may have put small candles on their cakes, possibly for religious reasons.

Birthday Pie!

Instead of a birthday cake,
many Russian children are
given a birthday pie!

Instead of using icing to spell a message,
Russian birthday pies have the
message carved into the pie crust.

Birthday Cards

The tradition of sending birthday cards
started in England about 100 years ago.
Originally cards were often sent
as an "apology" when a person
couldn't visit someone in person.

How Many Cards?

The average American receives eight birthday cards each year.

Lots of Cards!

Approximately

1.2 billion birthday cards

are given each year.

That special day

That special day you celebrate each year as your birthday isn't really your birth date. The actual day you were born slides around each year so that it lands on the following day of the previous year.

For example, if you were born on Saturday March 15th, the following year March 15th will fall on a Sunday, the year after on a Monday, and so on.

So how often do you celebrate the actual day you were born? Once every seven years!

Birthday dinner Out!

According to a survey, the most
popular day for eating out
in the United States is one's own
birthday—49 percent of American
adults eat out on their birthday.

HAPPY BIRTHDAY!

Most Official Birthday

George Washington is the
only man whose birthday is a
legal holiday in every state
of the United States.

"Everyman's Birthday"

In many countries, it is the custom to wish friends

"Happy Birthday!" on January 1 rather than "Happy New Year!"

This day is nicknamed "Everyman's Birthday,"

and is considered the day when everyone becomes a year older,

whether it's their actual day of birth or not.

In Good Company

On any given day,

more than 673,600 people

in the United States

are celebrating a birthday.

HAPPY BIRTHDAY!

FUN Birthday web Site

Visit this web site to find out where your birthday occurs in that never-ending number, pi.

http://www.facade.com/legacy/amiinpi/

What Happened on Your day?

Surf to this site to find out what happened in history on your birthday:

www.anydayinhistory.com

Happy Birthday, Bugs!

Bugs Bunny arrived into
the world on March 2, 1940,
in a cartoon called
"Elmer's Candid Camera."

Suffering Succotash!
It's My Birthday!

Daffy Duck burst onto

the screen on April 17, 1937,

in "Porky's Duck Hunt."

56

HAPPY BIRTHDAY!

Even Big Bird and
His Friends Have Birthdays!

Big Bird celebrates his
birthday on March 20th.

Oscar the Grouch celebrates
his birthday on June 1st.

HAPPY BIRTHDAY!

The Story of "Happy Birthday to You"

Two sisters, Mildred Hill, a teacher at the Louisville, Kentucky Experimental Kindergarten, and Dr. Patty Hill, the principal of the same school, wrote a song for the children, entitled "Good Morning to All." When Mildred combined her musical talents with her sister's expertise in the area of Kindergarten Education, "Good Morning to All" was sure to be a success.

The sisters published the song in 1893. Thirty-one years later, after Dr. Patty Hill became the head of the Department of Kindergarten Education at Columbia University's Teacher College, a gentleman by the name of Robert H. Coleman published the song without the sisters' permission. To add insult to injury, he added a second verse, the familiar "Happy Birthday to You."

Mr. Coleman's addition of the second verse popularized the song and, eventually, the sisters' original verse disappeared. "Happy Birthday to You," the one and only birthday song, had altogether replaced the sisters' original title, "Good Morning to All."

After Mildred died in 1916, Patty, together with a third sister named Jessica, sprang into action and took Mr. Coleman to court. In court, they proved that they, indeed, owned the melody. Because the family legally owned the song, it was entitled to royalties from it whenever it was sung for commercial purposes until they sold the rights.

First Song in Space

"Happy Birthday" was the first song

to be performed in outer space,

sung by the Apollo IX astronauts

on March 8, 1969.

Who Owns "Happy Birthday"?

Warner Communications paid $28 million for the copyright to the song "Happy Birthday." They are said to receive $2 million in royalties each year for commercial uses of the song.

PLAY "HaPPY BiRthDaY"
oN a touch-toNe PhoNe!

1 1 4 * 9 *
1 1 4 1 # 0
1 1 # 0 * 7 4
0 * 0 8

62

Golden Birthday

A "Golden Birthday" is the once-in-a-lifetime
day when you turn in years
the day of the month you were born.

For example, if you were born on April 16,
your "Sweet Sixteen" would also
be your "Golden Birthday."

Make Your Birthday Cake a Success

This website tells you how to troubleshoot your cake and make the next one come out perfectly. It will also tell you how to cut the one you have today with the right knife:

http://hersheykitchens.com/
baking_hints/cakes.asp

Who Shares a Birthday with You?

HAPPY BIRTHDAY!

Who shares a birthday with you in January?

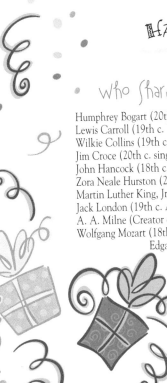

Humphrey Bogart (20th c. American actor)
Lewis Carroll (19th c. British mathematician and novelist, *Alice in Wonderland*)
Wilkie Collins (19th c. mystery writer, *The Woman in White*)
Jim Croce (20th c. singer, "Time in a Bottle")
John Hancock (18th c. American signer of Declaration of Independence)
Zora Neale Hurston (20th c. American novelist)
Martin Luther King, Jr. (20th c. American equal-rights reformer)
Jack London (19th c. Amercan novelist, *The Call of the Wild*)
A. A. Milne (Creator of Winnie the Pooh)
Wolfgang Mozart (18th c. Austrian composer)
Edgar Allen Poe (19th c. American short story writer and poet, *The Raven*)
Elvis Presley (20th c. American rock idol)
Jackie Robinson (20th c. American baseball player)
Franklin Roosevelt (U. S. president)
Betsy Ross (18th c. American revolutionary, sewed first official American flag)
Paul Revere (18th c. American revolutionary)
J.R.R. Tolkien (20th c. British fantasy writer, *The Hobbit*)
Last But not Least!
Arthur Conan Doyle's 19th c. fictional character, Sherlock Holmes

Birthday Thought to Make Your Year Bright!

Be such one, and live such a life, that if everyone such as you, and every life a life like yours, this earth would be God's paradise.

Birthday Scripture

Happy is everyone who fears the Lord, who walks in his ways.
You shall eat the fruit of the labor of your hands;
you shall be happy, and it shall go well with you.

Psalm 128:1-2 NRSV

HAPPY BIRTHDAY!

Who Shares a Birthday with You in February?

Susan B. Anthony (19th c. American suffragette)
Elizabeth Blackwell (19th c. American first woman physician in America)
Charles Dickens (19th c. British novelist, *David Copperfield*)
Thomas Edison (20th c. American inventer, light bulb)
Clark Gable (20th c. American actor, *Gone with the Wind*)
Galileo Galilei (16th and 17th c. Italian inventer and astronomer)
Horace Greeley (19th c. American journalist, "Go West, Young Man!")
Wilhelm Carl Grimm (19th c. German compiler of *Grimm's Fairy Tales* with his brother)
Langston Hughes (20th c. American poet)
Abraham Lincoln (U. S. president)
Henry Wadsworth Longfellow (19th c. American poet, *Evangeline*, "Song of Hiawatha")
Hannah More (19th c. British author and reformer)
Rosa Parks (20th c. American civil rights activist)
Ayn Rand (20th c. American philosopher)
Norman Rockwell (20th c. American painter)
Babe Ruth (20th c. American baseball player)
Adlai Stevenson Jr. (20th c. American statesman)
George Washington (U. S. president)
Simone Weil (20th c. French mystic)
Laura Ingels Wilder (20th c. children's writer, *Little House on the Prairie*)

Birthday Thought

Take care of the minutes,
and the hours will take care of themselves.

Birthday Scripture

Let us not become weary in doing good,
for at the proper time we will
reap a harvest if we do not give up.

Galatians 6:9 NIV

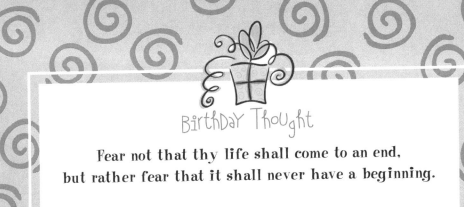

Birthday Thought

Fear not that thy life shall come to an end,
but rather fear that it shall never have a beginning.

Birthday Scripture

You have made known to me the path of life;
You will fill me with joy in your presence,
with eternal pleasures at your right hand.

Psalm 16:11 NIV

HAPPY BIRTHDAY!

Who Shares a Birthday with You in March?

Johann Sebastian Bach (18th c. German composer , "Jesu Joy of Man's Desiring")

Alexander Graham Bell (19th c. American inventor of the telephone)

Nat King Cole (20th c. American singer)

Albert Einstein (20th c. American theoretical physicist)

Ralph Ellison (20th c. American novelist, *The Invisible Man*)

Fannie Farmer (19th c. American writer of the first modern cookbook)

Aretha Franklin (20th c. American singer, "Respect")

Kenneth Graham (20th c. British children's writer, *The Wind in the Willows*)

Harry Houdini (20th c. American magician and writer)

James Madison (U. S. president)

Knute Rocke (20th c. American football coach)

Dr. Seuss (20th c. American children's writer, *The Cat in the Hat*)

Harriet Tubman (19th c. American civil war heroine of the underground railroad)

Vincent Van Gogh (19th c. Dutch painter, "Starry Night")

Sam Walton (20th c. American entrepreneur, Wal-mart)

Tennessee Williams (20th c. American playwright, *Cat on a Hot Tin Roof*)

HAPPY BIRTHDAY!

who shares a birthday with you in April?

Hans Christian Andersen (19th c. Danish writer of fairy tales)

Charlotte Bronte (19th c. novelist, *Jane Eyre*)

Elizabeth Barrett-Browning (19th c. British poet, "Songs of the Portuguese")

Charlie Chaplin (20th c. British silent film actor)

Daniel Defoe (18th c. British novelist, *Robinson Crusoe*)

Dorothea Dix (20th c. American reformer for the mentally ill)

Kurt Gödel (20th c. American mathmetician)

Billie Holliday (20th c. American blues singer)

Washington Irving (18th c. American writer, "Rip Van Winkle," "Legend of Sleepy Hollow")

Henry James (20th c. American Philosopher)

Thomas Jefferson (U. S. President)

Joseph Pulitzer (19th c. American jounalist and publisher)

William Shakespeare (16th c. English playwright, *Hamlet*)

Anthony Trollope (19th c. British novelist, *Barchester Towers*)

Booker T. Washington (19th c. American educator and founder of Tuskegee Institute)

Wilbur Wright (20th c. inventer of the airplane)

HAPPY BIRTHDAY!

Birthday Thought

I asked God for all things so I could enjoy life.
He gave me life so I could enjoy all things.

Birthday Scripture

If anyone is in Christ, he is a new creation;
The old has gone, the new has come.

2 Corinthians 5:17 NIV

HAPPY BIRTHDAY!

Who Shares a Birthday with You in May?

L. Frank Baum (19th c. American novelist, *The Wizard of Oz*)
Irving Berlin (20th c. American composer)
Nellie Bly (19th c. American journalist and reformer)
Edward Bulwer-Lytton (19th c. novelist, "It was a dark and stormy night.")
Rachel Carson (20th c. environmentalist and novelist, *Silent Spring*)
G. K. Chesterton (20th c. British Christian apologist)
Arthur Conan Doyle (19th c. mystery and science fiction writer, Sherlock Holmes stories)
Ralph Waldo Emerson (19th c. American transcendentalist poet)
Sigmund Freud (19th c. Austrian doctor and psychologist, father of psychoanalysis)
Julia Ward Howe (19th c. American composer, "The Battle Hymn of the Republic")
Calamity Jane (19th c. American adventurer and Indian scout under Wild Bill Hickok)
John Fitzgerald Kennedy (U. S. President)
Florence Nightingale (19th c. British reformer)
Katherine Anne Porter (20th c. American short story writer)
Dante Gabriel Rossetti (19th c. British pre-Raphealite painter)
Andrei Sakharov (20th c. Russian scientist)
Mary Shelley (19th c. novelist, *Frankenstein*)
Harry S. Truman (U. S. President)

Birthday Thought

The year's at the spring and day's at the morn:
Morning's at seven . . . God's in his heaven—
all's right with the world!

Birthday Scripture

Be grateful for the good things that the
LORD your God has given you and your family.

Deuteronomy 26:11 TEV

75

HAPPY BIRTHDAY!

Who Shares a Birthday with You in June?

Pearl S. Buck (20th c. American novelist)
Jack Dempsey (20th c. American boxer)
Anne Frank (20th c. German diarist)
Lou Gehrig (20th c. American baseball player)
Oscar Hammerstein II (20th c. playwright and composer, *Oklahoma*)
St. John of the Cross (16th c. Spanish mystic)
Helen Keller (20th c. writer)
Anne Morrow Lindbergh (20th c. American writer)
Marilyn Monroe (20th c. American film icon)
Blaise Pascal (16th c. French mathmetician and mystic)
George Orwell (20th c. British essayist and novelist, *Animal Farm*)
Richard Rogers (20th c. American playwright and composer)
Antoine de Saint-Exupery (20th c. pilot and poet, *The Little Prince*)
Dorothy L. Sayers (20th c. British scholar and novelist,
the Lord Peter Wimsey mysteries)
Johanna Spyri (20th c. children's author, *Heidi*)
Harriett Beecher Stowe (19th c. novelist, *Uncle Tom's Cabin*)
Igor Stravinski (20th c. Russian composer)

Birthday Thought

Just as a planet rushing through space is only a comet on its way to destruction until it is caught by some central sun and begins to revolve around that sun as its center and its life; so my life is an aimless comet burning itself out in its own self-will, till it finds the pull and attraction of Christ's love, halts its deadly way, and forever revolves around Him, its central sun and life.

Birthday Scripture

I am the way, and the truth, and the life.

John 14:6 NASB

77

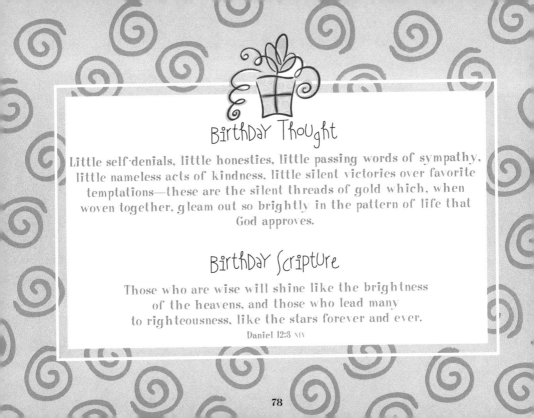

Birthday Thought

Little self-denials, little honesties, little passing words of sympathy, little nameless acts of kindness, little silent victories over favorite temptations—these are the silent threads of gold which, when woven together, gleam out so brightly in the pattern of life that God approves.

Birthday Scripture

Those who are wise will shine like the brightness of the heavens, and those who lead many to righteousness, like the stars forever and ever.

Daniel 12:3 NIV

HAPPY BIRTHDAY!

who Celebrates with You in July?

John Q. Adams (U. S. president)

P.T. Barnum (19th c. showman, Barnum-Bailey Circus)

Emily Jane Bronte (19th c. British novelist, *Wuthering Heights*)

Raymond Chandler (20th c. American mystery novelist, *The Maltese Falcon*)

George M. Cohan (20th c. American composer)

Princess Diana (20th c. British philanthropist)

Alexander Dumas (19th c. French novelist, *The Three Musketeers*, *The Count of Monte Cristo*)

Henry Ford (20th c. inventor of mass-produced cars, Model T Ford)

Helen Hayes (20th c. American actress)

Aldous Huxley (20th c. British essayist and novelist, *Brave New World*)

Estee Lauder (20th c. perfumier and cosmetic manufacturer)

Emmeline Parkhurst (20th c. American feminist reformer)

Beatrix Potter (20th c. British children's author, *Peter Rabbit*)

Rembrandt Van Rijn (17th c. Dutch painter)

E. B. White (20th c. American children's writer, *Charlotte's Web*)

HAPPY BIRTHDAY!

who shares a Birthday with You in August?

Louis Armstrong (20th c. American blues musician)
Lucille Ball (20th c. American television comedienne)
Ray Bradbury (20th c. American Science Fiction writer)
Coco Chanel (20th c. French couturier)
Francois Fenelon (17th c. French mystic)
Georgette Heyer (20th c. British romance writer)
Alfred Hitchcock (20th c. British filmmaker and writer)
Oliver Wendell Holmes (19-20th c. Supreme Court judge)
Lyndon B. Johnson (U. S. President)
T. E. Lawrence (20th c. explorer and writer, *Lawrence of Arabia*)
H. P. Lovecraft (20th c. American fantasy writer)
Grandma Moses (20th c. American painter)
Ogden Nash (20th c. American poet)
Dorothy Parker (20th c. American short story writer)
Sir Walter Scott (19th c. British novelist)
Alfred Lord Tennyson (19th c. British poet)
Mother Teresa (20th c. Roman Catholic founder of Missionaries of Charity)
Orville Wright (20th c. inventer of airplane)

HAPPY BIRTHDAY!

Thought for a Hot August Birthday!

There is no life so humble that, if it be true
and genuinely human and obedient to God,
it cannot reflect His light. There is no life
so meager that the greatest and wisest can
afford to despise it. We cannot know at what
moment it may flash forth with the life of God.

Birthday Scripture

Blessed are the meek:
for they shall inherit the earth.

Matthew 5:5

HAPPY BIRTHDAY!

who Celebrates with You in September?

Edgar Rice Burroughs (20th c. British novelist, *Tarzan*)
Miguel de Cervantes (17th c. Spanish novelist, *Don Quixote de la Mancha*)
Elizabeth I, Queen of England
Dame Agatha Christie (20th c. British mystery novelist)
Patsy Cline (20th c. American country singer)
Jesse Owens (20th c. American runner)
Ray Charles (20th c. American blues singer)
T. S. Eliot (20th c. British Poet)
James Fenimore Cooper (19th c. American novelist, *Last of the Mohicans*)
William Carlos Williams (20th c. American poet)
H. G. Wells (20th c. novelist "War of the Worlds")
Arthur Rackham (19th c. British illustrator)
Euripides (Greek playwright, b. 484 B. C.)
F. Scott Fitzgerald (20th c. American novelist, *The Great Gatsby*)
Kate Douglas Wiggins (20th c. American novelist, *Rebecca of Sunnybrook Farm*)
Upton Sinclair (19th c. American muckraker and novelist, *The Jungle*)

Birthday Thought

With the goodness of God to desire our highest welfare, the wisdom of God to plan it, and the power of God to achieve it, what do we lack?

Birthday Scripture

I can do everything through him who gives me strength.

Philippians 4:13 NIV

HAPPY BIRTHDAY!

Who Celebrates with You in October?

Aimee Semple McPherson (American evangelist)
Eleanor Roosevelt (President's wife and social reformer)
Jimmy Carter (American president)
Groucho Marx (Comedien)
Chubby Checkers (Singer, "Peppermint Twist")
Dwight Eisenhower (U. S. president)
Pablo Picasso (20th c. Spanish artist)
Theodore Roosevelt (U. S. president)
John Adams (U. S. president)
Graham Greene (British novelist)
Jonathan Edwards (18th c. theologian)
E. E. Cummings (20th c. American poet)
Katherine Mansfield (20th c. New Zealand short story writer)
Noah Webster (19th c. compiler of Webster's Dictionary)
Virgil (Roman poet, b. 70 B. C.)
Oscar Wilde (20th c. British playwright)
Arthur Miller (20th c. American playwright)
Samuel Taylor Coleridge (19th c. English poet)
Denise Levertov (20th c. American poet)

Birthday Thought

Without Christ life is as twilight with dark night ahead; with Christ it is the dawn of morning with the light and warmth of full day ahead.

Birthday Scripture

"I am the light of the world. Whoever follows me will never walk in darkness, but will have the light of life."

John 8:12 NIV

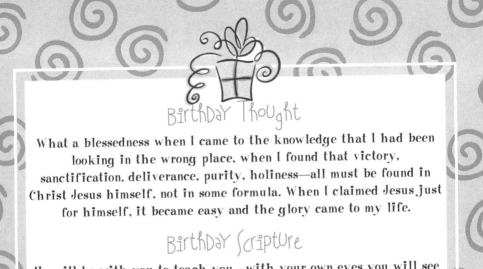

Birthday Thought

What a blessedness when I came to the knowledge that I had been looking in the wrong place, when I found that victory, sanctification, deliverance, purity, holiness—all must be found in Christ Jesus himself, not in some formula. When I claimed Jesus just for himself, it became easy and the glory came to my life.

Birthday Scripture

He will be with you to teach you—with your own eyes you will see your Teacher. And if you leave God's paths and go astray, you will hear a Voice behind you say, "No, this is the way; walk here."
Isaiah 30:20-21 TLB

HAPPY BIRTHDAY!

Who Shares Your Birthday in November?

Louisa May Alcott (19th c. American novelist, *Little Women*)

John Bunyan (17th c. English pastor and writer, *Pilgrim's Progress*)

Frances Hodgson Burnett (19th c. British novelist, *The Secret Garden*)

Marie Curie (20th c. Italian scientist and discoverer of radium)

Dorothy Day (20th c. American reformer)

Billy Graham (20th c. American evangelist)

Scott Joplin (19th c. American ragtime composer)

C. S. Lewis (20th c. British Christian Apologist, *Mere Christianity*, *Chronicles of Narnia*)

Astrid Lindgren (20th c. Swedish children's writer, *Pippi Longstocking*)

Margaret Mitchell (20th c. American novelist, *Gone with the Wind*)

Claude Monet (19th c. French impressionist painter)

Will Rogers (20th c. American humorist)

Robert Louis Stephenson (19th c. Scottish novelist, *Treasure Island*, "The Strange Case of Dr. Jekyll and Mr. Hyde")

Sojourner Truth (19th c. American abolitionist)

Mark Twain (19th c. American novelist and humorist, *Huckleberry Finn*)

HAPPY BIRTHDAY!

Who Shares a Birthday with You in December?

Jane Austin (19th c. novelist, *Pride and Prejudice*)

Clara Barton (19th c. American humanitarian, organised American Red Cross)

Ludwig Von Beethoven (19th c. German composer)

Evangeline Cory Booth (20th c. British General of the Salvation Army)

Emily Dickinson (19th c. American poet)

Walt Disney (20th c. American cartoonist, Mickey Mouse)

George MacDonald (19th c. Scottish Novelist, "The Light Princess")

John Milton (17th c. English poet, *Paradise Lost*)

Sir Isaac Newton (18th c. British mathematician)

Christina Rossetti (19th c. British poet)

Frank Sinatra (20th c. American singer, "I Did It My Way")

Aleksandr Solzhenitsyn (20th c. Russian novelist, *The Gulag Archipelago*)

James Thurber (20th c. American humorist)

Phillis Wheatley (19th c. American poet)

Woodrow Wilson (U. S. president)

Birthday Thought

The soul hardly realizes it,
but whether he is a believer or not,
his loneliness is really a homesickness for God.

Birthday Scripture

Pour out your hearts to him,
for God is our refuge.

Psalm 62:8 NIV

And there is healing in old trees

Old streets a glamour hold.

Why may not I as well as these,

Grow lovely growing old.

What Happened Then in Your Birthday Month?

What Happened Then in January?

Caesar crosses the Rubicon, 49 B.C.

Joan of Arc born (c.1412).

W.H. Fox Talbot produces first photographic negative, 1839

Shogunate abolished in Japan, 1868.

Victoria proclaimed Empress of India, 1877.

Treaty of Versailles ratified in Paris, 1920.

First United Nations General Assembly held in London, 1946

Vietnam War cease-fire signed, 1973

Birthday Moral for January

For each, God has a different response.

With everyone he has a secret—
the secret of a new name.

In everyone there is a loneliness, an inner chamber
of peculiar life which only God can enter.

"Before I formed you in the womb I knew you, before
you were born I set you apart. . . . I am with you."

Jeremiah 1:5-8 NIV

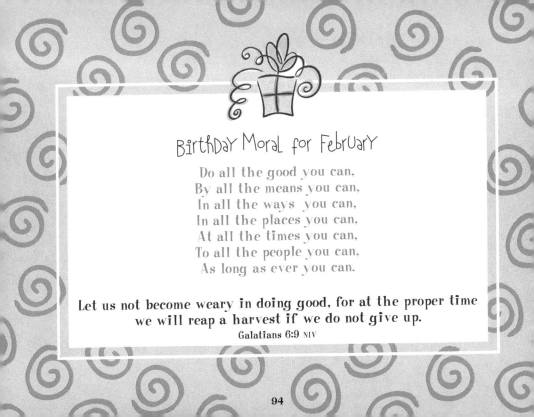

Birthday Moral for February

Do all the good you can,
By all the means you can,
In all the ways you can,
In all the places you can,
At all the times you can,
To all the people you can,
As long as ever you can.

Let us not become weary in doing good, for at the proper time we will reap a harvest if we do not give up.
Galatians 6:9 NIV

What Happened Then in February?

Diocletian declares a general persecution of Christians, 303

Earthquake at Lisbon kills 30,000 persons, 1531

Mary Queen of Scots executed, 1587

Rescue of Alexander of Selkirk (the real "Robinson Crusoe"), 1709

Pilgrim's Progress published, 1678

Captain Cook crosses the Antarctic Circle, 1773

"The Battle Hymn of the Republic" was first published in "Atlantic Monthly" as an anonymous poem, 1862

Feb 22, Hawaii became a US territory, 1900

"There she is..." The first Miss America was crowned in New York City, 1919

The first "micro on a chip" was patented by Texas Instruments, 1978

HAPPY BIRTHDAY!

What Happened Then in March?

Vasco da Gama discovers Mozambique, 1498

First daily paper (Courant) appears in England, 1703

Congress approved $30,000 to test camels for military use, 1855

Emancipation Edict liberates Russian serfs, 1861

Free city delivery of mail was authorized by the U.S. Postal Service, 1863

U.S. purchases Alaska from Russia, 1867

First intelligible sentences transmitted by Bell on the telephone, 1876

First woman member admitted to British House of Lords, 1922

Mohandas Gandhi begins civil disobedience campaign, 1930

Hollywood premiered "King Kong" in New York featuring Fay Wray, 1933

First automatic street light installed in New Milford, CT, 1949

Compact Disc recordings, developed by Phillips and Sony, were introduced, 1983

Birthday Moral For March

Love is not getting, but giving;
not a wild dream of pleasure,
and a madness of desire—
oh, no, love is not that—
it is goodness, and honor, and peace and pure living.

**"Greater love hath no man than this,
that a man lay down his life for his friends."**

John 15:13

HAPPY BIRTHDAY!

What Happened Then in April?

Petrarch crowned Poet on the Capital, Rome, 1341

Joan of Arc inspires French troops to victory at Orleans, 1429

Martin Luther excommunicated by Diet of Worms, 1521

Mutiny on the Bounty (the real one, not the movie), 1789

USA purchased Louisiana from France, 1803

Firing on Fort Sumter beginning U.S. Civil War, 1861

San Francisco earthquake and fire, 1906

S.S. Titanic sank, 1912

Harriet Quimby first woman to fly over English Channel, 1912

U.S. enters World War I, 1917

League of Nations founded, 1919

North Atlantic Treaty (NATO) signed in Washington, 1949

The space shuttle Challenger roared into orbit on its maiden voyage, 1983

First U.S. female into space, Sally Ride, 1983

Birthday Moral For April

**Be this our wall of bronze,
to have no guilt at heart,
no wrongdoing to turn us pale.**

Unto the pure all things are pure.

Titus 1:15

HAPPY BIRTHDAY!

What Happened Then in May?

Joan of Arc burned at the stake at Rouen, 1431

First permanent English settlement at Jamestown, 1607

Peter Minuit buys Manhattan from Indians, 1626

Union of England and Scotland as Great Britain, 1707

Benjamin Franklin's "Join or Die," the first newspaper cartoon is published, 1754

Order of the Legion of Honor created, 1802

Morse sends first message on U.S. telegraph line, 1844

Queen Victoria proclaimed Empress of India, 1876

The first horseless carriage show in London featured 10 models, 1896

Charles Lindbergh completes first solo nonstop flight across Atlantic, 1927

Explosion of the Hindenburg, 1937

First American hydrogen bomb dropped over Bikini atoll, 1956

South Africa chose Nelson Mandela to be the country's first black president, 1994

Birthday Moral for May

Never cease loving a person and never give up
hope for him, for even the Prodigal son
who had fallen most low could still be saved.
The bitterest enemy and also one who was
your friend could again be your friend;
love that has grown cold can kindle again.

**Dear friends, since God so loved us,
we also ought to love one another.**

1 John 4:11 NIV

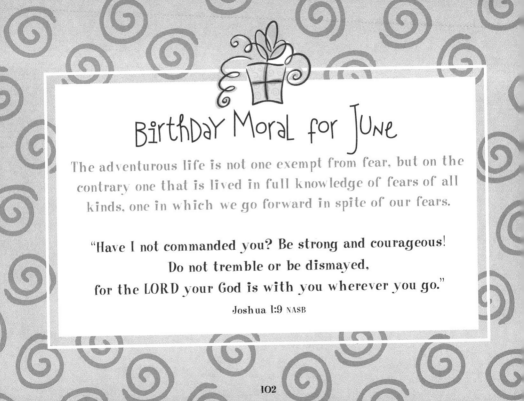

Birthday Moral for June

The adventurous life is not one exempt from fear, but on the contrary one that is lived in full knowledge of fears of all kinds, one in which we go forward in spite of our fears.

"Have I not commanded you? Be strong and courageous!
Do not tremble or be dismayed,
for the LORD your God is with you wherever you go."

Joshua 1:9 NASB

What Happened Then in June?

Magna Carta signed, 1215

First fire balloon ascent by Montgolfier Brothers, 1783

Reign of Terror begins in France, 1793

Alcock and Brown make first transatlantic flight, 1919

Atlantic Cable laid, 1858

Archduke Francis Ferdinand assassinated at Sarajevo, 1914

Treaty of Versailles signed, 1919

The first trade show at Atlantic City Convention Center featured electric light, 1929

U.S. intervenes in Korean War, 1949

87-foot memorial to Crazy Horse by Ziolkowski in S. Dakota dedicated, 1998

HAPPY BIRTHDAY!

What Happened Then in July

Vasco da Gama leaves Portugal to find way to India, 1497

Sir Thomas More executed, 1535

Spanish Armada destroyed, 1588

Declaration of Independence, 1776

The U. S. Military Academy opened its doors at West Point, New York,1802

George Stephenson constructs first effective steam locomotive, 1814

Revolution breaks out in Paris, 1830

Ben Franklin and George Washington on first U.S. government postage stamps, 1847

First Women's Rights Convention at Seneca Falls, N.Y., 1848

Perry opens up Japan, 1853

Pres. Theodore Roosevelt sends a message around the world in 12 minutes via Pacific Cable, 1903

"Pay-as-you-go" income tax withholding began, 1943

The U.S. Post Office inaugurated its five-digit ZIP codes, 1963

Hotmail, a free internet E-mail service began, 1996

Birthday Moral For July

But if I'm content with little,
Enough is as good as a feast.

**Godliness with contentment is
great gain. . . . having food and
raiment let us be therewith content.**

I Timothy 6:6,8

HAPPY BIRTHDAY!

What Happened Then in August?

Rome taken by the Huns, 410

Declaration of the Rights of Man adopted, 1789

Nelson wins Battle of the Nile, 1798

Lohengrin produced by Liszt at Weimar, 1850

First Atlantic cable completed, 1858

Germany invaded Belgium, 1914

Britain declares war on Germany, 1914

Opening of Panama Canal, 1914

Women's suffrage began in U.S., 1920

First atom bomb dropped on Hiroshima, 1945

The North Atlantic Treaty (NATO) went into effect, 1949

American Bandstand, hosted by Dick Clark, made its network debut,1957

Arthur Ashe is the first African-American to play on the U.S. Davis Cup tennis team,1964

Mark McGwire is the 16th person to hit 500-home runs, 1999

Birthday Moral For August

A sound mind in a healthy body is a short but full description
of a happy state in this world. He that has these two,
has little more to wish for; and he that wants either
of them, will be little the better for anything else.

Do not be wise in your own eyes;
Fear the LORD and depart from evil.
It will be health to your flesh, and strength to your bones.

Proverbs 3:7-8 NKJV

HAPPY BIRTHDAY!

What Happened Then in September?

Battle of Marathon, 490 B.C.

Mayflower set sail for America, 1620

Definitive Treaty of Peace signed ending American Revolution, 1783

Mexican revolt against the Spanish began, 1810

First cable sent from Britain to America, 1858

Bismarck delivers "Blood and Iron" speech, 1862

J.R.R. Tolkien's *The Hobbit* first published, 1937

Groundbreaking ceremony in N. Y. at the United Nations' world headquarters, 1948

The Miss America pageant made its network TV debut on ABC, 1954

The family drama series *The Waltons* premiered on CBS, 1972

9/11 NY City Trade Towers destruction unites world against terrorism, 2001

BirthDay Moral for September

Wisdom first teaches what is right.

**Wisdom is the principal thing;
Therefore get wisdom.
And in all your getting, get understanding.**

Proverbs 4:7 NKJV

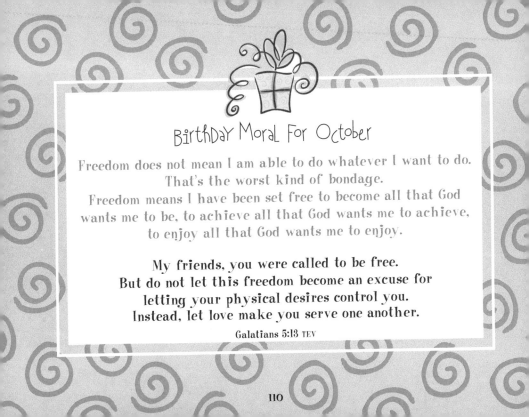

Birthday Moral For October

Freedom does not mean I am able to do whatever I want to do.
That's the worst kind of bondage.
Freedom means I have been set free to become all that God
wants me to be, to achieve all that God wants me to achieve,
to enjoy all that God wants me to enjoy.

**My friends, you were called to be free.
But do not let this freedom become an excuse for
letting your physical desires control you.
Instead, let love make you serve one another.**

Galatians 5:13 TEV

HAPPY BIRTHDAY!

What Happened Then in October?

Columbus touches land at Bahamas, 1492

Luther posts the 95 Theses at Augsburg, 1517

Tyndale burned at the stake, 1536

Special delivery mail service began in the United States, 1885

Statue of Liberty dedicated, 1886

Boer War begins, 1899

Orson Well's "War of the Worlds" broadcast panicked radio listeners who thought the
    simulated Martian invasion was real, 1938

The Mt. Rushmore sculpture was completed after 14 years of work, 1941

Little Golden Books (children books) began publishing, 1942

The situation comedy, *I Love Lucy*, premiered on CBS, 1951

Sputnik I launched, 1957

Nelson Mandela and F.W. de Klerk win Nobel Peace Prize for efforts to end apartheid, 1993

HAPPY BIRTHDAY!

What Happened Then in November?

Magellan sails into the Pacific, 1520

Drake begins circumnavigation of the world, 1577

Benjamin Franklin opens the first U.S. library, 1731

Stanley meets Livingstone at Ujiji, 1871

First ship sails through the Panama Canal, 1913.

Balfour Declaration promises a Jewish homeland, 1917

Armistice ends World War I, 1918

First Thanksgiving Parade held in Philadelphia, 1920

Limitation of Armaments Conference begins in Washington, 1921

King Tut's tomb discovered, 1922

Restoration of Williamsburg, Virginia begins, 1926

Woody Woodpecker debut in Walter Lantz's *Knock Knock*, 1940

"Are You Lonesome Tonight" by Elvis Presley #1 on the pop singles chart, 1960

Andrew Lloyd Webber's "Joseph & The Amazing Technicolor Dreamcoat" premiers, 1979

An iceberg, twice size of Rhode Island, sighted in Antarctic, 1987.

HAPPY BIRTHDAY!

Birthday Moral for November

Hope is like the sun which,
as we journey towards it,
casts the shadow of our burden behind us.

O my God, my soul is in despair within me;
Therefore I remember You from the land of the
Jordan and the peaks of Hermon, from Mount Mizar.
Deep calls to deep at the sound of Your waterfalls;
All Your breakers and Your waves
have rolled over me.

Psalm 42:6-7 NASB

HAPPY BIRTHDAY!

What Happened Then in December?

Mayflower landed, 1620

Cromwell becomes Lord Protector of the Commonwealth, 1653

Napoleon crowned Emperor by the Pope, 1804

Publication of Tennyson's "Charge of the Light Brigade," 1854

Lady Astor is first woman member of the House of Commons, 1919

Aswan Dam opened in Egypt, 1902

Wright brothers' first flight at Kitty Hawk, 1903

Roald Amundsen reaches South Pole, 1911

In an unofficial truce, German and English troops trade Christmas greetings and sing carols, 1914

Women first voted in British general election, 1918

King Edward VIII of England abdicates to marry Mrs. Simpson, 1936

Bombing of Pearl Harbor, 1941

United Nations International Children's Emergency Fund (UNICEF) established, 1946

Dr. Christiaan Barnard performs first heart transplant operation, 1967

Apollo 8 astronauts orbiting the moon read from Genesis during a Christmas Eve TV broadcast, 1968.

Challenger, the Lunar Lander for Apollo 17, touches down on the Moon's surface, 1972

Birthday Moral for December

**Prosperity is only an instrument to be used,
not a deity to be worshipped.**

Instruct those who are rich in this present world not to be conceited
or to fix their hope on the uncertainty of riches, but on God, who
richly supplies us with all things to enjoy. Instruct them to do good,
to be rich in good works, to be generous and ready to share, storing
up for themselves the treasure of a good foundation for the future,
so that they may take hold of that which is life indeed.

1 Timothy 6:17-19 NASB

MY time be in THY hand!

Perfect the cup as planned!

Let age approve of youth, and

Death complete the same!

HAPPY BIRTHDAY!

Traditions

Birthday Tree

One family celebrates birthdays in their home with
a tiny, white Christmas tree about twelve inches high.
First, they decorate the tree with handmade stars
and hearts in the birthday person's favorite colors.
The birthday gifts are placed on or under the tree.
Sometimes the tree is placed on top of the gifts.

A Special Plate

For one family, only on birthdays would a
beautiful red plate show up at the
dinner table at the place of the guest of honor.
On Christmas Day, this same plate lay
on the table at Christmas dinner in front
of an empty chair in honor of Jesus' birthday.

Birthday Blessing

As soon as they had blown out the candles
on their cake in one family, the father
would pray a special birthday prayer for
the birthday person, asking God to
bless them during the coming year.

Piñata

Although one large family didn't have much money,
the mother would always get a piñata, a brightly-
colored, hollow paper-maché animal, which she
would fill with candy and hang from a tree in the
backyard. The children would be blindfolded and
turned in a circle several times. Then, the guests
would sing songs while the birthday person tried to
break the piñata with a stick, releasing its goodies.

Easter Birthday Cake

One little girl's birthday fell near Easter. The year she was three, she made a wish before blowing out the candles: "I wish I could have a cake shaped like an Easter bunny every birthday for the rest of my life!" Even though she is now in her 30s, her mother has made her a bunny cake every year, complete with coconut sprinkles on white frosting, and gumdrops for the eyes, nose, mouth, and ears.

Special day

Many families treat birthdays as the birthday person's "special" day. On their birthday they can choose not only the flavor of the cake and ice cream but also the supper menu for that day and a special activity.

Celebration of Life

One woman lost her husband in an accident when he was only twenty-five years old. Every year since, his family and friends have come together on his birthday. They view this as an opportunity to celebrate his life and keep his memory fresh in their hearts and minds. It is always a positive and joyous occasion and keeps the family in touch.

"What Do Ya think this is?"

One fun-loving family has a funny tradition that has endured through the years. During the course of the day, each person looks for an opportunity to say to the birthday person, "Hey! What do ya think this is, your birthday?" They bombard the birthday person with that line all day long!

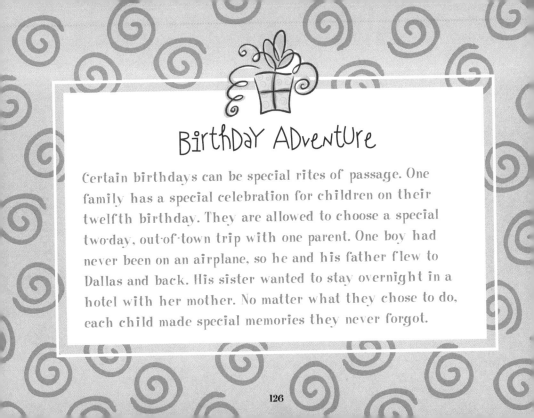

BirthDay ADVenture

Certain birthdays can be special rites of passage. One family has a special celebration for children on their twelfth birthday. They are allowed to choose a special two-day, out-of-town trip with one parent. One boy had never been on an airplane, so he and his father flew to Dallas and back. His sister wanted to stay overnight in a hotel with her mother. No matter what they chose to do, each child made special memories they never forgot.

"To Grow On"

Some families place
an extra candle on
the cake "to grow on."

Again!

In one family, everyone gets a chance
to celebrate. After the birthday person
has blown out the candles, they relight
them and sing a sped-up version of the
Happy Birthday song, while the very
young children are invited to take
a turn blowing out the candles.

HAPPY BIRTHDAY!

Activities
for Right Now

HAPPY BIRTHDAY!

Lip-Sync Fun

Gather old clothing, sunglasses, musical
instruments—anything useful for making
an interesting costume. Choose songs from
popular CDs, but don't let your
contestants know which song
they will lip-sync.

Once the music begins, the contestant
must quickly pull together an
appropriate costume and begin to perform.
Let the other guests' applause
determine the prizewinner.

Photo Scavenger Hunt

Use a 1-hour photo service with some disposable cameras or use digital cameras. Send the teams of party guests out on a scavenger hunt for photos of the following:

- Three people with two feet on the ground
- Giving an older person a hug
  - A picture of one person petting a live animal
  - Taking an escalator backwards

- A person performing a trick
- Standing in water
- Playing with children's toys
- One person smelling a flower
- Or make up your own fun list!

When the photos are gathered, let there be prizes for best, funniest, and most clever collections.

Gathering Memories

Grab a video camera. Have each guest
share a birthday greeting,
a meaningful memory about
the birthday person, or
a quality they admire.

Play it at the end of the party,
and present the tape as a gift
to the guest of honor! Make it
an annual tradition and let
past video messages be a part
of the party entertainment.

Birthday Scripture

Have everyone pick out a birthday

scripture for the birthday person.

Have them read it aloud and

explain why they chose it.

Most Meaningful Birthday

Go around the room and have

each guest share a story about

their most meaningful or

most memorable birthday.

HAPPY BIRTHDAY!

It wouldn't be complete without YOU!

Is someone missing from your gathering of
friends and family? Call them right now.
Give each guest a turn to visit,
and let your absent loved one
be part of your party.

Birthday Movies or Plays?

Hand around some pieces of paper
and see how many birthday movies,
plays, and pop tunes your guests
can come up with.

HAPPY BIRTHDAY!

True or False?

Have each person take a turn and share two true statements and one false one about their past birthdays. Have the others try to guess which is the false statement.

Mystery Person

Pass out pieces of paper and have each
guest write something about themselves,
a birthday experience if they wish, that
no one in the room knows. Have them each
fold up their paper and put it in a bowl.
Draw out one of the papers and read it aloud.
Have everyone try to guess who wrote it.

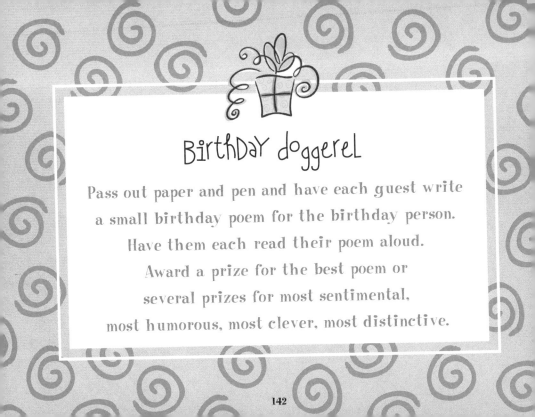

Birthday doggerel

Pass out paper and pen and have each guest write
a small birthday poem for the birthday person.
Have them each read their poem aloud.
Award a prize for the best poem or
several prizes for most sentimental,
most humorous, most clever, most distinctive.

HAPPY BIRTHDAY!

Activities
For Future Birthdays

Photo Finish Party

Don't let the guest of honor be the only one chided about aging! Have the guests bring a personal baby photo. Collect the photos at the door and spread them on a table with numbers under each one. (You may want to add a few unrelated baby photos to make the game more difficult!) Then, have guests write down which photos they believe belongs to which guest. The winner receives a baby bottle filled with candy or a disposable camera.

Happy Birthday Across the Miles

Is the birthday person far away from family and friends? Have a party, complete with cake and gifts. Videotape the party, allowing each guest to send a greeting. Have a proxy blow out the candles on camera, and take group pictures of the celebration. Send the videotape with gifts, phone numbers of those present, and a phone card.

HAPPY BIRTHDAY!

Phone Party

For this kind of a party, you need a speaker phone.
As the party-goers arrive, a call is put in to the
birthday person. The party begins and the
birthday person is included via the telephone.
Gifts could be sent ahead of time so the person
could unwrap the gifts over the
phone and thank the givers.
Another variation would be to use a
computer and a digital camera at
both locations for a video conference.

Happy Birthday All Year Round

For a friend in a nursing home or assisted living quarters,
buy a twelve-month calendar with pockets. In each
pocket place treats to be used that month, such as a
bookmark, seasonal greeting card with a message
inside from you, a tea bag or cocoa packet, and an
inspirational pamphlet or small paperback book.

HAPPY BIRTHDAY!

One-Year-Older Tea

For a ladies' birthday party, give a semi-formal
tea party. Have each person come to tea with her
favorite tea cup and saucer or mug for drinking tea.
Bring out various teas in porcelain and stoneware
teapots. Serve the traditional tea foods like finger
sandwiches and nut breads on trays in the
living room. Give fancy tea prizes
for most unusual, prettiest, and
funniest tea cup or mug.

Hats, Hats, Hats Party

Ask your guests to arrive at the party wearing hats.
These can be funny, elaborate, absurd, and
even sentimental. They can include everything
from swim caps to Easter bonnets to military
berets. During the party, the guests line up
and each models his or her hat for the
birthday honoree, who then gives prizes for:
"Overall Favorite", "Most Unique",
"Best Looking", "Most Endearing", etc.

Praise they that will times past,

I joy to see myself now live.

This age best pleases me.

Celebrating Your
Spiritual Birthday

Spend the entire Day with god.

Gather up your Bible, a journal to write in, three sack meals, music and something to play it on. Go to a special place—a park, your back yard, a lonely beach—someplace you can be alone, uninterrupted with God. Talk to Him about the year and write down insights that come to you in prayer. Spend time just being with Him—don't feel you have to talk all day. Read. Sing. Be still. Enjoy His company.

Throw a Party

Invite friends to come help you celebrate
your Spiritual Birthday. Ask each one to
bring a Bible verse or encouraging thought
to help you through the coming year.
Tell them about the day you became a
Christian and what led up to it. Have each
of your guests share their verse or thought.

HAPPY BIRTHDAY!

Thanking Those Who Helped You Grow

Spend some time on your special day writing thank-you notes to the people who most helped you to grow in your spiritual life. Let them know what they did and what effect it had on your life.

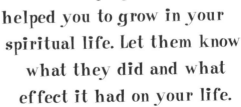

Autograph Page

Have your birthday guests sign their names below:

A Prayer of Blessing for Your Birthday

Happy birthday! May you be blessed today as we celebrate your life and what you mean to us! May it be a day as special as you are, filled with all of your favorite things, and may it be the beginning of the best year you've known yet.

May you put past adversity and pain behind you, while holding the memory of good things closely to your heart. May you look forward with anticipation to the days ahead, trusting that God is at work in your life to bless you.

May you experience wholeness and a sense of well-being in your spirit, your soul, and your body. May your heart be filled with God's love, and may that love fill any empty spot you feel inside. As you are filled to overflowing, may He use you to pass His love on to others.

May God's peace guard your mind to shield you from stress and fear, and may His joy fill your days with singing. And as you enjoy the warmth of His presence, may He grant you your heart's desire.

Amen.

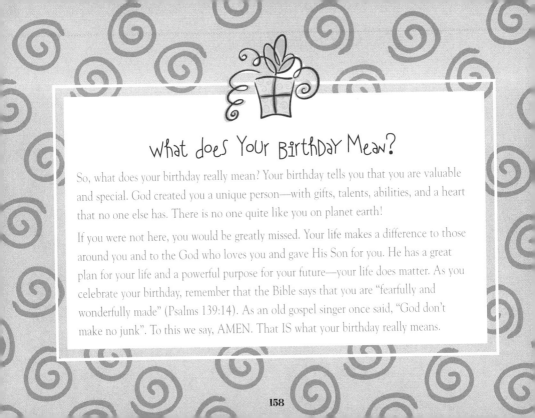

what does Your BirthDay Mean?

So, what does your birthday really mean? Your birthday tells you that you are valuable and special. God created you a unique person—with gifts, talents, abilities, and a heart that no one else has. There is no one quite like you on planet earth!

If you were not here, you would be greatly missed. Your life makes a difference to those around you and to the God who loves you and gave His Son for you. He has a great plan for your life and a powerful purpose for your future—your life does matter. As you celebrate your birthday, remember that the Bible says that you are "fearfully and wonderfully made" (Psalms 139:14). As an old gospel singer once said, "God don't make no junk". To this we say, AMEN. That IS what your birthday really means.

Acknowledgements

Hans Christian Anderson (8), William Wordsworth (10,17), Dwight L. Moody (11), Orlando A. Battista (12), Charles Hadden Spurgeon (13), Bernard Baruch, On his eighty-fifth birthday (14), Sir Arthur Kent (15), William Blake (16), Corrie ten Boom (18), Anonymous (19,26,31,35,73, 95), P. K. Shaw (20), Ronald Reagan, On his sixty-sixth birthday (21), Anthony J. d'Angelo (22), Alexander Maclaren (23), Bob Hope (24), Ben Franklin (25), Maurice Chevalier (27), Robert Louis Stevenson (28), P. J. Bailey (29), Soren Kierkegaard (30,101), Arnold Glasgow (32), Michel de Montaigne (33), Edward Bulwer Lytton (34), Thomas Jefferson (36), Philips Brooks (67), Lord Chesterfield (69), John Henry Newman (71), Robert Browning (75), E. Stanley Jones (77), Frederic William Farrar (79), Phillip Brooks (81), A. W. Tozer (83), Philip Schaff (85), A. B. Simpson (87), Hubert Van Zeller (89), Karle Wilson Baker (90), George MacDonald (93), Henry Van Dyke (97), Horace (99), Paul Tournier (103), Isaac Bickerstaffe (105), John Locke (107), Juvenal (108), Warren W. Wiersbe (111), Samuel Smiles (113), Calvin Coolidge (115), Robert Browning (116), Robert Herrick (150).

If you have enjoyed this book, or if it has
impacted your life, we would like to hear from you.
Please contact us at:

Honor Books
An Imprint of Cook Communications Ministries
4050 Lee Vance View
Colorado Springs, CO 80918
www.cookministries.com